When You Don't Know What to Say

When You Don't Know What to Say

Words of Caring for All Occasions

SECOND EDITION

WRITTEN AND COMPILED BY
Doris Rikkers

DISCOVERY HOUSE
PUBLISHERS®

Discovery House Publishers is affiliated with RBC Ministries,
Grand Rapids, Michigan.

Scripture quotations are from the HOLY BIBLE, NEW
INTERNATIONAL VERSION®, NIV® . Copyright © 1973, 1978,
1984 by Biblica, Inc.™ Used by permission of Zondervan. All
rights reserved worldwide. www.zondervan.com

Interior design by Sherri L. Hoffman

Printed in the United States of America

Fourth Printing 2011

Contents

Getting Started

Welcome to this expanded edition of *When You Don't Know What to Say*. Since the first edition of this volume was published in 2007, it has become a popular resource for many. Now, building on the original material, we have added a number of new categories, additional sentiments to existing categories, plus a new record-keeping feature.

There was a time when the written word was the only means of communicating with people over long distance. Modern innovations like text messaging, e-mails, and cell phones have made communication easier and faster, but, as a result, handwritten messages have become a rare treasure. When someone actually takes the time to send a note or write a letter, it becomes more meaningful, more personal, and more permanent. It becomes a record of thoughts and sentiments that can be revisited and cherished time and again.

We want to help you show your family, friends, acquaintances, and others who may cross your path how much you care by taking the time to write. To feed the soul of a friend or loved one who may be celebrating one of life's joyous events or struggling through a time of difficulty.

Proverbs 25:11 tells us that "a word spoken in right circumstances" is "like apples of gold in settings of silver." Yet many people struggle with finding "just the right words" to say "in right circumstances." So we want to help you get started by providing you with some appropriate sentiments and Scriptures in this book. We've also included some of our favorite devotional thoughts from some of our favorite authors.

Whether you want to wish your neighbor a happy birthday or offer a message of support to that person at church who is struggling with the loss of a loved one, the process is as easy as looking through this volume and finding the right category. When you do, you will find a variety of messages. Choose the one that suits the situation best, and use it to bless another person with the right words. Mix and match sentiments and Scriptures as you think appropriate. Or use the sentiments here as a springboard to create your own message—sometimes just the right prompt can get your own creative juices flowing!

However you choose to use these "right words," we are sure that those who receive them will be encouraged to know that you have cared enough to take the time to write.

უ

As an additional feature, in this new edition each sentiment has a small number beside it. You can use this number to record when you have used it and to whom you sent it on the Record of Sentiments Sent page at the end of each topic.

Genuine Love

*W*e can easily describe what it feels like to "be loved," but we have trouble translating that into what it means to "be loving." We feel loved when someone wants to be with us, takes the risk of letting us know him, takes the time to get to know us, and always does what is in our best interest. Our desire to be on the receiving end of this kind of devotion is much greater than our ability to return it.

To be loved is one of the strongest of all desires. The need for love is as much a part of God's design for humans as the need for air, water, and food. We can't lead a healthy life without it . . . One of the ways God passes along His love is through others, generally those closest to us. . . .

The Bible describes love in this familiar New Testament passage:

> Love is patient, love is kind. It does not envy, it does not boast, it is not proud. It is not rude, it is not self-seeking, it is not easily angered, it keeps no record of wrongs. Love does not delight in evil

but rejoices with the truth. It always protects, always trusts, always hopes, always perseveres.

—1 Corinthians 13:4–7

In other words, love seeks the highest good. God's love is perfect because He seeks the highest good for all creation. Every human being longs to be the recipient of this kind of love, but no human can provide it. The only place to experience genuine love is in a relationship with the One whose very being defines it. Not only is God the perfect example of love, He *is* love, and apart from His love for us none of us could love or be loved.

We love because he first loved us.

—1 John 4:19

☙

JULIE ACKERMAN LINK
The Art of Loving God

Appreciation

We are so thankful for your contribution. 1
Please accept our deepest appreciation for all
you do.

> *And whatever you do, whether in*
> *word or deed, do it all in the name of*
> *the Lord Jesus, giving thanks to God*
> *the Father through him.*
> COLOSSIANS 3:17

. . . .

In appreciation and thanks. 2
We just want to let you know how much we
appreciate all you do for our church.
God bless you and keep you strong as you continue
to serve others.

> *This service that you perform is not*
> *only supplying the needs of God's*
> *people but is also overflowing in many*
> *expressions of thanks to God.*
> 2 CORINTHIANS 9:12

☐ 3 Weeks and months pass and you continue to work
         tirelessly for others.
     Although you may not always be aware of it,
     I do notice your contribution and deeply appreciate
         all that you do.

> *How can we thank God enough for you*
> *in return for all the joy we have in the*
> *presence of our God because of you?*
> 1 THESSALONIANS 3:9

❧ APPRECIATION ❧
Record of Sentiments Sent

Note No.	Sent to:	Date

Birthday

❏ 1   Today is a day to celebrate YOU!
Have a happy day
   and a year full of wishes
      come true.
Happy Birthday

> *I thank my God every time I*
> *remember you. In all my prayers*
> *for . . . you, I always pray with joy.*
> PHILIPPIANS 1:3–4

.... ✄ ....

❏ 2   To a wonderful friend
   on your birthday—
Sending lots of wishes that your day will be filled
   with delightful moments,
And your year will overflow
   with God's blessings.
Happy Birthday

> *Teach us to number our days aright,*
> *that we may gain a heart of wisdom.*
> PSALM 90:12

A Birthday Blessing
3 ☐
    God's grace be with you,
    His peace surround you,
    His love enfold you
    On your birthday and always.
Happy Birthday

> *Grace to you and peace*
> *from God our Father and*
> *the Lord Jesus Christ.*
> PHILEMON 3

.... ♫ ....

Wishing you a birthday
4 ☐
    that is filled with all things
    you count as special:
        Good friends,
        Dear family,
        And joy to last all year.

> *The joy of the Lord*
> *is your strength.*
> NEHEMIAH 8:10

5 Birthdays are reminders to rejoice!
Your life is worth celebrating because you are so
special.

> *May the righteous be glad*
> *and rejoice before God;*
> *may they be happy and joyful.*
> PSALM 68:3

.... ॐ ....

6 You are one of a kind,
so rejoice and celebrate
your special day.
Happy birthday!

> *The Lord your God is with you,*
> *he is mighty to save.*
> *He will take great delight in you,*
> *he will quiet you with his love,*
> *he will rejoice over you with singing.*
> ZEPHANIAH 3:17

This day is like no other—it's your birthday! 7 🗌
You are like no one else—you're unique!
Now that's something to celebrate!
Happy Birthday to you!

> *He will yet fill your mouth with laughter*
> *and your lips with shouts of joy.*
> JOB 8:21

.... ߱ ....

May your day and the year ahead be filled with 8 🗌
sweet joy and laughter.
Happy Birthday!

> *Light is shed upon the righteous*
> *and joy on the upright in heart.*
> PSALM 97:11

❏ 9   Best wishes to a very special person
       on a very special day.
   Happy birthday to YOU!

> *You love righteousness*
> *and hate wickedness;*
> *therefore God, your God,*
> *has set you above your companions*
> *by anointing you with the oil of joy.*
>
> <small>PSALM 45:7</small>

.... ॐ ....

✌ BIRTHDAY ✌

Record of Sentiments Sent

Note No.	Sent to:	Date

——Congratulations——

❏ 1   Congratulations on your latest achievement.
I knew you could do it!

> *And whatever you do, whether*
> *in word or deed, do it all in the*
> *name of the Lord Jesus, giving*
> *thanks to God the Father*
> *through him.*
> COLOSSIANS 3:17

....

❏ 2   Congratulations on your promotion!
May your success continue each day
in your new position.

> *Teach me to do your will,*
> *for you are my God;*
> *may your good Spirit lead me*
> *on level ground.*
> PSALM 143:10

Celebrate!
You've worked hard to reach
   this new level of achievement.
I'm so proud of you!

> *That everyone may eat and drink,*
> *and find satisfaction in all his toil—*
> *this is the gift of God.*
> ECCLESIASTES 3:13

.... ⌘ ....

Congratulations for using your gift of leadership.
May God bless you in all you do.

> *May the favor of the Lord our*
> *God rest upon us;*
> *establish the work of our hands for us—*
> *yes, establish the work of our hands.*
> PSALM 90:17

☐ 5 Your latest achievement makes you shine!
Let's celebrate!

> *May the righteous be glad*
> *and rejoice before God;*
> *may they be happy and joyful.*
> PSALM 68:3

.... ↝ ....

☐ 6 May God's love, justice, and peace shine through
you as you assume
this new responsibility.

> *And now, O Israel, what does the Lord*
> *your God ask of you but to fear the Lord*
> *your God, to walk in all his ways, to love*
> *him, to serve the Lord your God with all*
> *your heart and with all your soul.*
> DEUTERONOMY 10:12

Go with God's blessing as you take on your new
   level of responsibility.

> *Whoever serves me must follow
> me; and where I am, my servant
> also will be. My Father will
> honor the one who serves me.*
> JOHN 12:26

. . . . ꒜ . . . .

God's hand has guided you to this level of
   accomplishment.
Seek His wisdom as you continue on the path of
   success.

8 ☐

> *Commit to the Lord whatever you do,
> and your plans will succeed.*
> PROVERBS 16:3

ॐ CONGRATULATIONS ॐ
Record of Sentiments Sent

Note No.	Sent to:	Date

Graduation

Graduation brings pride and joy for past
   accomplishments
   and excitement for the future
     that lies ahead.
Congratulations
   on your graduation.

1

> *"For I know the plans I have for you,"*
> *declares the Lord, "plans to prosper you*
> *and not to harm you, plans to give you*
> *hope and a future."*
> JEREMIAH 29:11

On your graduation,
   may God richly bless you
     in all you do.

2

> *May he give you the desire of your heart*
> *and make all your plans succeed.*
> PSALM 20:4

☐ 3   As you graduate
            and face whatever life may bring,
        may God's hand guide
            your every step.

> *In his heart a man plans his course,*
> *but the Lord determines his steps.*
> PROVERBS 16:9

.... ✍ ....

☐ 4   Congratulations
        on your graduation!
    Great challenges lie ahead.
        Great opportunities
            are before you.
        Go in God's grace and love
            as your future unfolds.

> *I can do everything*
> *through him who gives me strength.*
> PHILIPPIANS 4:13

Congratulations
   on your graduation!
Whatever your future holds,
   Wherever your life takes you,
   God's gracious hand
      will guide you.
   His love will surround you.

> *Be strong and courageous . . .*
> *for the Lord your God will*
> *be with you wherever you go.*
> JOSHUA 1:9

.... ༈ ....

✑ GRADUATION ✑
Record of Sentiments Sent

Note No.	Sent to:	Date

Military

May God's guidance and protection be with you
    as you serve our country.

> *Be careful, keep calm*
> *and don't be afraid.*
> ISAIAH 7:4

. . . .

God's love will surround you,
    and His peace will enfold you
        wherever you go.
May God bless you as you serve in the military.

> *The LORD himself goes before you and*
> *will be with you; he will never leave you*
> *nor forsake you.*
> DEUTERONOMY 31:8

3   Our prayers and thoughts are with you.

Whether you're stateside or stationed overseas,
      you'll be in our thoughts.
Whether you're deployed for a few months or
      several years,
      you will remain in our hearts always.
May God bless you in all you do.

> *Be strong and courageous. Do not*
> *be terrified; do not be discouraged,*
> *for the LORD your God will be*
> *with you wherever you go.*
> JOSHUA 1:9

4   As you serve in the military, remember this:
      You will be in our thoughts each day,
      You will be in our hearts forever.
      And God will be with you wherever you go.

> *Jesus said, "I am with you always…"*
> MATTHEW 28:20

Though days will pass and things may change, 5 ☐
    remember this:
We will always be proud of you.
We will always love you.
We will hold you close in our thoughts and
    prayers.

> *The LORD bless you and keep you;*
> *the LORD make his face shine*
> *upon you and be gracious to you;*
> *the LORD turn his face toward*
> *you and give you peace.*
> NUMBERS 6: 24–26

.... ૐ ....

As you go to serve our country, you may be far 6 ☐
    from us,
But you will always be close in our hearts
    and constantly in our thoughts and prayers.

> *May you be blessed by the LORD,*
> *the Maker of heaven and earth.*
> PSALM 115:15

❑ 7   We are so proud that you have chosen to serve
in the military.
May God protect and guide you in all you do.

> *For I am convinced that neither death*
> *nor life, neither angels nor demons,*
> *neither the present nor the future, nor*
> *any powers, neither height nor depth,*
> *nor anything else in all creation, will be*
> *able to separate us from the love of God*
> *that is in Christ Jesus our Lord.*
>
> ROMANS 8:38–39

. . . . ⌇ . . . .

❑ 8   God bless you as you serve in the military.
Be assured that our sovereign Lord is in control
of all things.

> *Be still, and know that*
> *I am God.*
> *I will be exalted*
> *in the earth.*
>
> PSALM 46:10

God will protect you and give you strength.
Trust Him to guide you as you serve our country
overseas.

> *Be strong in the Lord and*
> *in his mighty power.*
> EPHESIANS 6:10

.... ✦ ....

❧ MILITARY ❧
Record of Sentiments Sent

Note No.	Sent to:	Date

Pastors and Ministry Staff

You have been such a joy and blessing to our congregation.
Thank you for your Christlike witness.

> *This service that you perform is not only*
> *supplying the needs of God's people but is also*
> *overflowing in many expressions of thanks to*
> *God. Because of the service by which you have*
> *proved yourselves, men will praise God for the*
> *obedience that accompanies your confession of*
> *the gospel of Christ, and for your generosity in*
> *sharing with them and with everyone else.*
> 2 CORINTHIANS 9:12–13

❑ 2   We have seen Christ's love and compassion through
you.
Thank you for all you have done to make the
fellowship of this church so special.

> *Each one should use whatever gift*
> *he has received to serve others,*
> *faithfully administering God's*
> *grace in its various forms.*
> 1 PETER 4:10

.... ᔓ ....

❑ 3   With prayers and best wishes
for many more years of serving in Christ's
kingdom.

> *You did not choose me, but I chose you*
> *and appointed you to go and bear*
> *fruit—fruit that will last.*
> *Then the Father will give you*
> *whatever you ask in my name.*
> JOHN 15:16

I'm so glad you have chosen to minister to our
congregation.
Your preaching and pastoral care have touched
us all.

4 □

> *Be shepherds of God's flock that is under your
> care, serving as overseers—not because you
> must, but because you are willing, as God wants
> you to be; not greedy for money, but eager to
> serve; not lording it over those entrusted to you,
> but being examples to the flock. And when the
> Chief Shepherd appears, you will receive the
> crown of glory that will never fade away.*
> 1 PETER 5:2–4

.... ༄ ....

Following a call to serve the Lord as a pastor is a
wonderful testament of your faith.
God bless you richly as you serve Him in the years
ahead.

5 □

> *Then I heard the voice of the Lord
> saying, "Whom shall I send?
> And who will go for us?"
> And I said, "Here am I. Send me!"*
> ISAIAH 6:8

☐ 6　Your preaching inspires us,
　　　Your caring renews us,
　　　Your counsel brings us God's peace.
　　　Thank you for sharing the gospel message and
　　　　　Christ's love with us.

> *Those who have served well gain an*
> *excellent standing and great assurance*
> *in their faith in Christ Jesus.*
> 1 TIMOTHY 3:13

································ ⟫ ································

☐ 7　Through your life and your ministry you have
　　　　shown us Christ's love,
　　　　the Father's mercy,
　　　　and the Spirit's joy.
　　　Thank you for leading our congregation.

> *Now he who supplies seed to the sower*
> *and bread for food will also supply and*
> *increase your store of seed and will enlarge*
> *the harvest of your righteousness.*
> 2 CORINTHIANS 9:10

Your music ministry has brought joy to our hearts.

Thank you for making each service so special with your gift of music.

> *I always thank God for you because of his grace given you in Christ Jesus.*
> 1 CORINTHIANS 1:4

8

.... ✦ ....

You have a special calling to teach our children and young people.

Thank you for being an example of Christ's faithfulness.

Thank you for showering our children with Christ's love.

9

> *May the God of hope fill you with all joy and peace as you trust in him, so that you may overflow with hope by the power of the Holy Spirit.*
> ROMANS 15:13

❏ 10 You have been a great blessing to our congregation.
May God richly bless you as you continue to serve
Him.

> *My grace is sufficient for you, for my*
> *power is made perfect in weakness.*
> 2 CORINTHIANS 12:9

.... ᘒ ....

❧ PASTORS AND MINISTRY STAFF ❧
Record of Sentiments Sent

Note No.	Sent to:	Date

Welcome to Our Church

❏ 1

Welcome to our church!
I'm so glad you chose to be part of our church
family.

> *Live in harmony with one another;*
> *be sympathetic, love as brothers,*
> *be compassionate and humble.*
> 1 PETER 3:8

❏ 2

May you find a warm welcome, sincere hearts, and
joyful fellowship in your new church home.
Welcome!

> *Accept one another, then,*
> *just as Christ accepted you,*
> *in order to bring praise to God.*
> ROMANS 15:7

Welcome to our church!

3

I hope you find this to be a place of
   great fellowship,
      sound teaching,
         and joyful worship.

> *How good and pleasant*
> *it is when God's people*
> *live together in unity!*
> PSALM 133:1 (TNIV)

.... ✦ ....

4

We give you a warm welcome.
What a delight to have your family join us in
   fellowship.
May you feel God's presence as you worship with us.

> *Come, let us bow down in worship,*
> *let us kneel before the Lord our Maker.*
> PSALM 95:6

☐ 5   May God's grace and peace enfold you as you join
         our church fellowship and worship with us.
      Welcome!

> *Grace and peace to you from God our*
> *Father and the Lord Jesus Christ.*
> 1 CORINTHIANS 1:3

.... ౨ ....

☙ WELCOME TO OUR CHURCH ❧
Record of Sentiments Sent

Note No.	Sent to:	Date

New Home and —Welcome to the— Neighborhood

☐ 1 May God's presence surround you in your new
home.

> *The Lord blesses the home of the righteous.*
> PROVERBS 3:33

☐ 2 I'm so glad you moved into our neighborhood!
Right now I only know you as "neighbor,"
but soon I hope to call you "friend."

> *Therefore, as God's chosen people,*
> *holy and dearly loved, clothe yourselves*
> *with compassion, kindness, humility,*
> *gentleness and patience.*
> COLOSSIANS 3:12

Whether you moved across town or across the 3 ☐
country,
We hope you feel welcomed by our caring and
friendship.
Welcome to our neighborhood!

> *Do everything in love.*
> 1 CORINTHIANS 16:14

.... ᘍ ....

Welcome neighbors! 4 ☐
If there is anything you need to make moving in
more manageable and less frantic,
please feel free to ask.
We would love to help.

> *Dear children, let us not*
> *love with words or tongue but*
> *with actions and in truth.*
> 1 JOHN 3:18

☐ 5 Enjoy your new home!
We hope you find a warm welcome from everyone
in your new neighborhood.

Serve one another in love.
GALATIANS 5:13

························ ᔓ ·······························

☐ 6 There's nothing like a good neighbor
who chats with you over the fence or over
coffee,
who runs an errand or watches the kids
for just a minute,
who provides a cup of sugar or a stick of butter.

I'd love to be your good neighbor, so please ask.
I'm glad to help in any way I can.

*If you really keep the royal law found
in Scripture, "Love your neighbor as
yourself," you are doing right.*
JAMES 2:8

I'm so glad your family has chosen our
   neighborhood.
I'm sure you will find a warm welcome here.

> *Love does no harm to its neighbor.*
> *Therefore love is the fulfillment of the law.*
> ROMANS 13:10

.... ✒ ....

❧ WELCOME TO THE NEIGHBORHOOD ❧
Record of Sentiments Sent

Note No.	Sent to:	Date

Looking for Comfort

I often quote Psalm 27 to encourage people who are going through a difficult time. The psalmist was living in very unpleasant circumstances, yet he expected to "see the goodness of the Lord in the land of the living" (v. 13). But I now have many friends who are ill or bedridden with no prospect of getting better. How can they find comfort in these words?

We could emphasize the truth that our ultimate hope resides not in this present life but in the world now unseen, our future home in heaven (2 Corinthians 4:18; 5:1–8). Even though that is true, it seems that the psalmist was speaking of an expectation in this present world, "in the land of the living," rather than the next world.

So let's look more closely at the psalmist's hope. His expectation was not necessarily deliverance from bad circumstances but the hope of seeing "the goodness of the Lord." That's something we can see even in times of trouble.

When my friend Maurice was hospitalized due to a stroke from which he was told he would never totally recover, he said to me, "While flat on my back, I have been thinking about God. I sense His goodness and greatness as never before."

No matter what your situation, you can find evidence of God's goodness—so keep looking for it with hope.

୬

HERB VANDER LUGT
Our Daily Bread

Comfort

May the Father of compassion   1
and the God of all comfort
surround you with love.

> *Praise be to the God and Father*
> *of our Lord Jesus Christ,*
> *the Father of compassion and*
> *the God of all comfort,*
> *who comforts us in all our troubles.*
> 2 CORINTHIANS 1:3–4

....

To comfort you—   2
May good friends surround you,
God's love enfold you,
and the Spirit's presence
bring you peace.

> *You will keep in perfect peace*
> *him whose mind is steadfast,*
> *because he trusts in you.*
> ISAIAH 26:3

❏ 3   In our time of need
          the Spirit surrounds us
             with His love
          and fills our hearts with peace.

> *Cast your cares on the Lord*
> *and he will sustain you;*
> *he will never let the righteous fall.*
> PSALM 55:22

························· ⌁ ·························

❏ 4   In this difficult time
          may the peace of the Spirit
             fill your heart,
          the love of the Father
             renew your strength,
          and the promise of the Savior
             bring you hope.

> *Jesus said, "I have told you these things,*
> *so that in me you may have peace.*
> *In this world you will have trouble.*
> *But take heart! I have overcome the world."*
> JOHN 16:33

The God of all comfort

　supplies us with—

　　　strength to face today,
　　　hope to face tomorrow,
　　　and peace to face the future.

> *The Lord gives strength*
> *to his people;*
> *the Lord blesses his people*
> *with peace.*
> PSALM 29:11

5 ☐

······························ ☽ ····························

May the love of Christ

　comfort you in this difficult time and
　bring you peace.

> *I will never leave you*
> *nor forsake you.*
> JOSHUA 1:5

6 ☐

7   Through the darkest hours,
      the longest nights,
      the loneliest moment,
      God's love will surround you,
      His strength will uphold you,
      His peace will fill your heart.

He gives strength to the weary and
increases the power of the weak.
Isaiah 40:29

8   Comfort comes in many ways—
      a thoughtful prayer,
      a gentle smile,
      a loving hug.

Be kind and compassionate
to one another.
Ephesians 4:32

God has promised:
    Though grief may
    overshadow you,
        it will not consume you.
    Though sorrow fills your soul,
        it will fade away.

Thinking of you during this difficult time.

> *This I call to mind and*
> *therefore I have hope:*
> *Because of the Lord's great love*
> *we are not consumed,*
> *for his compassions never fail.*
> *They are new every morning;*
> *great is your faithfulness.*
> LAMENTATIONS 3:21–23

································· ᔓ ·································

Although your world is shaken,
    God stands firm and
        holds you fast
            in His loving arms.

> *The eternal God is your refuge, and*
> *underneath are the everlasting arms.*
> DEUTERONOMY 33:27

❧ COMFORT ❧
Record of Sentiments Sent

Note No.	Sent to:	Date

Encouragement

God is good—all the time!
May you be encouraged by these words
   and find a new perspective on what is
   happening just now.

> *Surely goodness and love will follow me*
> *all the days of my life,*
> *and I will dwell in the house of the Lord*
> *forever.*
> PSALM 23:6

May your heart find comfort in the memories of
      the past
   and hope in the promises of the future.

> *May you be blessed by the Lord,*
> *the Maker of heaven and earth.*
> PSALM 115:15

☐ 3   Look around you:
      there is always something to be thankful for.

> *Give thanks to the Lord, for he is good;*
> *his love endures forever.*
> 1 Chronicles 16:34

.... ⌒ ....

☐ 4   Give thanks to God for He is good . . .
      all the time!
  Focus your mind on the joys of today.
  Find strength in knowing that God is in
      control of everything.

> *The eternal God is your refuge, and*
> *underneath are the everlasting arms.*
> Deuteronomy 33:27

May you be encouraged to know that our Sovereign 5 ☐ Lord is in control.

Nothing can happen without His knowledge and will.

> *Be still, and know that I am God;*
> *I will be exalted among the nations.*
> *I will be exalted in the earth.*
>
> PSALM 46:10

.... ✎ ....

ENCOURAGEMENT
Record of Sentiments Sent

Note No.	Sent to:	Date

Friendship

I took a moment today
   to think of you
and thank God for your
   enduring friendship.
Thank you for being
   such a great friend.

A friend loves at all times.
PROVERBS 17:17

. . . .

Just wanted to let you know
   I've been blessed with thoughts of you
and our friendship.

A happy heart
makes the face cheerful.
PROVERBS 15:13

3   Through gales of laughter,
        Through tears of sorrow,
        Through times I couldn't face alone,
            You were there for me.
        Thank you so very much.
        Your friendship
            means everything to me.

I thank my God
every time I remember you.
PHILIPPIANS 1:3

································· ᔐ ·································

4   Good friends stand with you
        on the mountaintop and applaud.
    Best friends walk with you
        through the valley
        and hold your hand.
    Thanks for being my best friend.

Two are better than one . . .
If one falls down,
his friend can help him up.
ECCLESIASTES 4:9–10

Having you for a friend
    has added an abundance
        of joy to my life.
What a blessing you are.

Dear children, let us not love
with words or tongue
but with actions and in truth.
1 JOHN 3:18

································ ··· ································

❧ FRIENDSHIP ❧
Record of Sentiments Sent

Note No.	Sent to:	Date

—Praying for You—

I just want you to know that I am praying for you
as you journey through this difficult time in
your life.

> *May the grace of the Lord Jesus Christ,*
> *and the love of God, and the fellowship*
> *of the Holy Spirit be with you all.*
> 2 CORINTHIANS 13:14

I am praying that you will find God's peace,
comfort, and hope in the days ahead.

> *Therefore, since we have been justified*
> *through faith, we have peace with God*
> *through our Lord Jesus Christ.*
> ROMANS 5:1

❏ 3   You are being upheld in our thoughts
        and supported with our prayers.
        May knowing this give you strength to face the
            future.

> *Surely God is my salvation;*
> *I will trust and not be afraid.*
> *The Lord, the Lord, is my strength and*
> *my song; he has become my salvation.*
> ISAIAH 12:2

.... ❧ ....

❏ 4   Be strengthened by knowing that we are all praying
        for you.

> *We always thank God,*
> *the Father of our Lord Jesus Christ,*
> *when we pray for you.*
> COLOSSIANS 1:3

Daily we lay our requests in prayer at Jesus' feet.   5 ☐
Daily our thoughts of you are lifted to heaven.
May you find strength in knowing that so many of
    us care.

> *For he will command his angels*
> *concerning you to guard*
> *you in all your ways.*
> PSALM 91:11

.... ↝ ....

In trust we turn to God in prayer.   6 ☐
In confidence we wait for God's answer.
By faith we know that He will do whatever is best
    for us.

> *Do not be anxious about anything,*
> *but in everything, by prayer*
> *and petition, with thanksgiving,*
> *present your requests to God.*
> PHILIPPIANS 4:6

❧ PRAYING FOR YOU ❧
Record of Sentiments Sent

Note No.	Sent to:	Date

Thank You

Thank you for your kindness.
  You have shown me God's love.

1 ☐

> *God is love. Whoever lives in love*
> *lives in God, and God in him.*
> 1 JOHN 4:16

.... ⌘ ....

God has showered me
  with blessings through you.
Thank you for all you've done
  to help me through
    this difficult time.

2 ☐

> *Let us encourage one another.*
> HEBREWS 10:25

☐ 3 Your thoughtfulness
        means so much to me.
    Thank you for your kind words,
        your caring actions,
        your constant prayers.

> *He who does what is right*
> *is righteous, just as he is righteous.*
> 1 JOHN 3:7

····························· ✑ ·····························

☐ 4 I thank God every day
        that He has sent you
            into my life.
    Thank you for your thoughtfulness and caring.

> *Dear friends,*
> *let us love one another,*
> *for love comes from God.*
> *Everyone who loves has been*
> *born of God and knows God.*
> 1 JOHN 4:7

"Thank you" is such a small phrase to express my 5 ☐
   feelings
      for all you've done.
Your willingness to help
   was greatly appreciated.

As we have opportunity,
let us do good to all people.
GALATIANS 6:10

.... ૐ ....

Thank you for all you do. 6 ☐
You have made a corner of my world
   a very special place to be.

I always thank God for you because of
his grace given you in Christ Jesus.
1 CORINTHIANS 1:4

7 So many times you have done wonderful things
for others.
Now you have done wonderful things for me.
Thank you for caring.

I thank my God every time
I remember you.
PHILIPPIANS 1:3

.... ᧡ ....

8 Thank you! Thank you! Thank you!
Your caring came at just the right time when I
needed you most.

We always thank God, the Father
of our Lord Jesus Christ,
when we pray for you.
COLOSSIANS 1:3

You are so special!
Thank you for being there when I needed a friend
with a warm hug and a smile.

> *You will be made rich in every way so*
> *that you can be generous on every*
> *occasion, and through us your generosity*
> *will result in thanksgiving to God.*
> 2 Corinthians 9:11

.... ↝ ....

Your friendship means the world to me.
Thank you for making me feel so special.

> *A friend loves at all times.*
> Proverbs 17:17

∽ THANK YOU ∾
Record of Sentiments Sent

Note No.	Sent to:	Date

The Rx for Laughter

"A cheerful heart is good medicine"
—Proverbs 17:22

*I*t's been rough," my friend said, "but I've finally made it through!" We were celebrating the completion of a miserable, but necessary, year of chemotherapy in her battle against cancer.

She leaned back and looked at me thoughtfully. "You'll never know how much I appreciated all those cards, notes, and letters you sent to me day after day."

I laughed and told her that she *should* appreciate them since I'm usually the world's most inconsistent letter-writer. But I explained that God had assigned me "mailbox duty" that year. And along with the assignment He gave me an unusual sense of eagerness and joy about it, so if the letters had helped she should thank *Him.*

"Well, the love and encouragement kept me going," she said. "But do you know what I appreciated more than anything else in those letters? Those funny, silly things you wrote that made me *laugh*. Because at a time like that, just when it's most needed, laughter is the hardest to find."

Truly, laughter is a gift that we can give to one another—a gift meant to be shared. Laughter, joy, and just plain fun have a way of building strength into friendships. Laughter creates memories. It is life's bubbles and often its best medicine. And strips of shining laughter weave friendship's basket tight enough to hold the tears.

> A happy heart makes the face cheerful, but heartache crushes the spirit . . . All the days of the oppressed are wretched, but the cheerful heart has a continual feast . . . A cheerful look brings joy to the heart, and good news gives health to the bones.
>
> —Proverbs 15:13, 15, 30

> However many years a man [woman] may live, let him [her] enjoy them all. But let him [her] remember the days of darkness, for they will be many.
>
> —Ecclesiastes 11:8

I know that there is nothing better for men [women] than to be happy and do good while they live.

—Ecclesiastes 3:12

৯

SUSAN LENZKES
Crossing the Bridge Between You and Me

Get Well

□ 1 While you get well . . .
      May God's love bring you comfort,
      His promises bring you peace,
      His faithfulness bring you hope.

> *The Lord will sustain him*
> *on his sickbed*
> *and restore him*
> *from his bed of illness.*
> PSALM 41:3

. . . .

□ 2 This little note
      brings words of cheer
      and my hope that you are better soon.

> *And the God of all grace . . .*
> *will himself restore you*
> *and make you strong.*
> 1 PETER 5:10

A prayer for your recovery:
    May God's arms enfold you,
    His peace surround you,
    His loving hands heal you.

I am the Lord, your God,
who takes hold of your right hand and
says to you, Do not fear;
I will help you.
ISAIAH 41:13

.... ෨ ....

As you wait to get well,
    Be patient.
    God is working day by day
      to restore your strength,
      renew your spirit
      and return you to complete health.

Those who hope in the Lord
will renew their strength.
They will soar
on wings like eagles;
they will run and not grow weary,
they will walk and not be faint.
ISAIAH 40:31

☐ 5   We do not know why we are asked to endure pain
and sickness.
What we do know is that God will stand by our
side and see us through.
May you feel God's presence as He brings you
back to health.

> *The Lord is faithful to all his promises*
> *and loving toward all he has made.*
> PSALM 145:13

.... ꝑ ....

☐ 6   Just wanted to let you know—
I'm hoping
you get stronger each day
and are soon feeling better.
Get well soon.

> *Be strong and take heart,*
> *all you who hope in the Lord.*
> PSALM 31:24

❧ GET WELL ❧
Record of Sentiments Sent

Note No.	Sent to:	Date

——Thinking of You——

☐ 1   Thinking of you and praying
       that God's blessings
          will be showered upon you throughout your
          day.

> *My God will meet all your needs*
> *according to his glorious riches*
> *in Christ Jesus.*
> PHILIPPIANS 4:19

☐ 2   My mind is filled
       with happy thoughts—all of you.
       Just wanted to let you know
          you brought a smile to my day.

> *I thank my God*
> *every time I remember you.*
> PHILIPPIANS 1:3

Thinking of you 3 ☐
  and praying you will be renewed by God's
    presence.

> *He gives strength to the weary*
> *and increases the power of the weak.*
> ISAIAH 40:29

.... ॐ ....

Thinking of you 4 ☐
  and praying God's peace
    will fill your heart and mind.

> *You [O Lord]*
> *will keep in perfect peace*
> *him whose mind is steadfast,*
> *because he trusts in you.*
> ISAIAH 26:3

❑ 5 Just wanted to say—
       I'm hoping this little note of cheer
          brings a smile to your face
             and laughter to your life.

                          May the God of hope fill you
                              with all joy and peace
                                as you trust in him.
                                       ROMANS 15:13

.... ᘓ ....

❑ 6 Just wanted you to know . . .
       I thought of you today
       And it filled my day with joy.

                              I have not stopped
                             giving thanks for you,
                      remembering you in my prayers.
                                      EPHESIANS 1:16

Today was such a lovely day, 7
Though skies were dark and clouds were grey.
My morning thoughts were all of you—
As those at noon and evening too.
Thus the sun shone bright, the sky was blue
Because my mind was set on you.

> *This is the day the Lord has made;*
> *let us rejoice and be glad in it.*
> PSALM 118:24

.... ᧿ ....

May the blessings of the Father, 8
   The joy of the Son,
      And the peace of the Holy Spirit
Dwell in you, now and for many years to come.
Thinking of you in a special way.

> *God . . . is my witness how constantly*
> *I remember you.*
> ROMANS 1:9

☐ 9 Today, marked as routine, was full of surprises,
        flashing colorful memories of moments we
            knew.
    The tone of your laughter filled the air all around me,
        and my thoughts were all of you.

> *I thank my God every time I remember you.*
> PHILIPPIANS 1:3

> *We always thank God, the Father of our
> Lord Jesus Christ, when we pray for you,*
> COLOSSIANS 1:3

❧ THINKING OF YOU ❧
Record of Sentiments Sent

Note No.	Sent to:	Date

Serious Illness

❧

☐ 1 God is with you always.
His love surrounds you,
His hand is upon you,
He will uphold you with His mighty arm
  and His presence will give you peace.

> *May the God of hope fill you with all*
> *joy and peace as you trust in him,*
> *so that you may overflow with hope*
> *by the power of the Holy Spirit.*
> ROMANS 15:13

.... ॐ ....

☐ 2 God's love surrounds you each moment of your day.
His peace guards you through the long hours of the
  night.
His comfort will be with you always.
May you feel God's presence and perfect peace.

> *Come to me, all you who are weary and*
> *burdened, and I will give you rest.*
> MATTHEW 11:28

We do not know what tomorrow will bring,
But we do know this:
   God's plan is perfect,
      His grace abounds
         and He provides only what
            is the very best for us.
May you rest in God's providence and peace.

> *I am the LORD, your God, who takes*
> *hold of your right hand and says to you,*
> *Do not fear; I will help you.*
> ISAIAH 41:13

.... ✍ ....

❧ SERIOUS ILLNESS ❧
Record of Sentiments Sent

Note No.	Sent to:	Date

Remembering What God Has Done

❧

Throughout Scripture God emphasizes the importance of remembering, and He encourages the use of memory devices. One of the first examples is found in the first book of the Bible. God placed a rainbow in the sky to remind himself of His promise to never again destroy all life with a flood (Genesis 9:13–16).

Many years later when Moses addressed six hundred thousand recently freed slaves and their families, he told the people to use memory devices to help them remember the commandments God had given to them.

> Tie them as symbols on your hands and bind them on your foreheads. Write them on the doorframes of your houses and on your gates.
>
> —Deuteronomy 6:8–9

God told the Israelites to remember such things as: the Sabbath (Exodus 20:8); the things you have seen (i.e., what God has done) (Deuteronomy 4:9); that God brought them out of slavery (Deuteronomy 5:15); the

Lord, His laws, His decrees (Deuteronomy 8:11); that God is God and there is no other (Isaiah 46:9).

To help people remember, God established an assortment of holiday celebrations during which the people were to stop working and take time to remember and enjoy everything God had done for them (see Leviticus 23).

All religious holidays are in fact memory devices. Christians have a set of holidays to remember the life and work of Christ.

※

JULIE ACKERMAN LINK
Loving God with All My Mind

Thanksgiving

Happy Thanksgiving
1 ☐
   With grateful hearts
      we gather together
   and give thanks to God
      for our bounty of blessings.
   Wishing you and your loved ones
      a blessed Thanksgiving.

> *Give thanks to the Lord, for he is good;*
> *His love endures forever.*
> PSALM 118:1

. . . . ॐ . . . .

With grateful hearts
2 ☐
   we give thanks to God
   for family and friends,
   for home and health
      and happiness.
Have a blessed Thanksgiving Day.

> *You are my God, and I will give you thanks;*
> *you are my God, and I will exalt you.*
> PSALM 118:28

❏ 3   Thinking of you at Thanksgiving
At Thanksgiving I thank God
    for all He has given me—
    especially for friends like you.
Have a blessed Thanksgiving, my friend.

Enter his gates with thanksgiving
and his courts with praise;
give thanks to him and praise his name.
For the Lord is good and his love
endures forever.
PSALM 100:4

.... ✺ ....

❏ 4   On this day of thanksgiving,
    We remember God's blessings
        and give Him thanks:
For our home, our health,
    our family, our friends,
    our freedom.
Have a wonderful
    Thanksgiving Day.

How great you are,
O Sovereign Lord!
There is no one like you,
and there is no God but you.
2 SAMUEL 7:22

❧ THANKSGIVING ❧
Record of Sentiments Sent

Note No.	Sent to:	Date

Christmas

☐ 1 Into a world of darkness He came . . .
    The Prince of Peace
    The King of Glory
    The Hope of the World
Let us rejoice!

> *For God so loved the world*
> *that he gave his one and only Son,*
> *that whoever believes in him*
> *shall not perish but have eternal life.*
> JOHN 3:16

.... ⅔ ....

☐ 2 Just as the angels sang
    to announce Christ's birth,
Let us sing the songs of Christmas
    and tell the world of God's love.
Have a blessed Christmas.

> *Sing and make music*
> *in your heart to the Lord.*
> EPHESIANS 5:19

With joy we welcome
   the coming of Christ
      and celebrate
      this holy time of year.
   May you have
      a blessed Christmas season.

> *For to us a child is born,*
> *to us a son is given.*
> ISAIAH 9:6

·· ···

Be joyful and sing.
   Christ has come
      to bring joy to the world.
Have a blessed Christmas
   and a joyous New Year.

> *Light has come into the world.*
> JOHN 3:19

❏ 5   Music fills the world
      with the songs of Christmas.
  Rejoice and sing—
      our Savior is born!

> *Today in the town of David*
> *a Savior has been born to you;*
> *he is Christ the Lord.*
> LUKE 2:11

.... ༄ ....

❏ 6   Merry Christmas

    May Christmas bring you
      blessings of family and friends.

    May your New Year be filled
      with God's goodness.

> *The Lord has done great things for us,*
> *and we are filled with joy.*
> PSALM 126:3

℈ CHRISTMAS ℈
Record of Sentiments Sent

Note No.	Sent to:	Date

Easter

☐ 1   This Easter,
      may you know Mary's thrill
      at hearing the words:
      "He is not here. He is risen!"
   Happy Easter

> *The angel said . . . "He is not here; he*
> *has risen, just as he said."*
> MATTHEW 28:5–6

☐ 2   At Easter and always
      may the announcement
       "He Lives"
      fill your heart with joy.

> *Praise be to the God and Father of our Lord*
> *Jesus Christ! In his great mercy he has given*
> *us new birth into a living hope through the*
> *resurrection of Jesus Christ from the dead.*
> 1 PETER 1:3

Christus lives . . .
 To rule over our lives
 And reign supreme
  in our world.

> *Thanks be to God!*
> *He gives us the victory*
> *through our Lord Jesus Christ.*
> 1 CORINTHIANS 15:57

.... ॐ ....

Christ is risen! Hallelujah!
 Christ's resurrection
 floods our lives
  with hope and joy.
 Have a blessed Easter.

> *Christ Jesus . . . has destroyed death*
> *and has brought life and immortality*
> *to light through the gospel.*
> 2 TIMOTHY 1:10

ᔥ **Easter** ᔥ
Record of Sentiments Sent

Note No.	Sent to:	Date

Caught Off Balance

"For I am the Lord your God, who takes hold of your right hand and says to you, Do not fear; I will help you."

—Isaiah 41:13

Sudden loss, besides leaving us hurt and bewildered, can leave us listing seriously to one side. This state of imbalance is surprising, if not downright frightening. We had no idea we were leaning so heavily on a person, job, or ability until it was yanked away without warning.

When a loved one who partially defines who we are (or who we are *not*) is taken away by death, distance, divorce, or disagreement, our grief is intensified by the loss of this part of ourselves. Maybe we had depended on the person to express emotion for us or to think or decide for us. Perhaps the person was our sense of humor, our planner, our conscience, our practical side, our memory, or even our proof of worth. In one way or another, that person was our *balance*. And now we are *off* balance.

It is not just the loss of a person that can throw us off balance. Sometimes the loss of a job, ability, ideal, attribute, or goal carries with it a large chunk of our self-esteem, identity, or purpose, leaving us feeling lopsided and ready to topple over. When this happens, it may be time to confess that our sense of well-being was improperly anchored. We may also discover that our vision needs to expand—that who we are is more than what we do or how we look, and that the sum of our worth is far more than any loss.

God's secure love and His sure promise to care for us are the perfect ballast; they provide stability without adding weight to our load. When our lives are filled with Jesus Christ and the security, worth, and identity He provides, the losses we experience cannot destabilize us.

We may still toss and turn in stormy weather, but we'll never run aground or be shipwrecked.

Find rest, O my soul, in God alone; my hope comes from him. He alone is my rock and my salvation; he is my fortress, I will not be shaken. My salvation and my honor depend on God; he is my mighty rock, my refuge. Trust in him at all times, O people; pour out your hearts to him, for God is our refuge.

—Psalm 62:5–8

I waited patiently for the Lord; he turned to me and heard my cry. He lifted me out of the slimy pit, out of the mud and mire; he set my feet on a rock and gave me a firm place to stand. He put a new song in my mouth, a hymn of praise to our God. Many will see and fear and put their trust in the Lord. Blessed is the man who makes the Lord his trust, who does not look to the proud, to those who turn aside to false gods.

—Psalm 40:1–4

SUSAN LENZKES
When Life Takes What Matters

Apology

☐ 1 Sometimes I speak before I think.
I'm so sorry that what I said hurt you.
Please accept my apology.

> *Forgive me this wrong!*
> 2 CORINTHIANS 12:13

· ·

☐ 2 I'm sorry my words and actions made you feel
uncomfortable.
Please forgive me for my thoughtlessness.

> *I appeal to you, brothers, in the name of*
> *our Lord Jesus Christ, that all of you agree*
> *with one another so that there may be no*
> *divisions among you and that you may be*
> *perfectly united in mind and thought.*
> 1 CORINTHIANS 1:10

Occasionally I don't realize that my mouth outpaces 3 ☐
  my mind.
Please forgive me for my careless use of words.
I never meant to hurt your feelings.

> *Be kind and compassionate to*
> *one another, forgiving each other,*
> *just as in Christ God forgave you.*
> EPHESIANS 4:32

.... ☙ ....

I'm sorry I wasn't completely truthful. 4 ☐
Please forgive me.

> *Let the peace of Christ rule in your*
> *hearts, since as members of one*
> *body you were called to peace.*
> COLOSSIANS 3:15

❏ 5   I hope you can find it in your heart to forgive me.
I never meant to damage our friendship.
I'm sorry.

> *Bear with each other and forgive whatever*
> *grievances you may have against one*
> *another. Forgive as the Lord forgave you.*
> COLOSSIANS 3:13

APOLOGY
Record of Sentiments Sent

Note No.	Sent to:	Date

Sympathy

□ 1   You are in my thoughts and prayers as you grieve
your loss.
God bless you and keep you close in your time of
sadness.

> *For I am the Lord, your God, who*
> *takes hold of your right hand and says*
> *to you, Do not fear; I will help you.*
> ISAIAH 41:13

□ 2   Through your tears
and in your sorrow,
know that God holds you close.

> *Be still and know that I am God.*
> PSALM 46:10

Tears will come
   and grief may consume us,
      but we have hope.
The day is coming
   when death's pain
      will be no more.

> *He will swallow up death forever.*
> *The Sovereign Lord will wipe away*
> *the tears from all faces.*
> ISAIAH 25:8

.... ☙ ....

Faith is our comfort as we grieve.
   May your faith
      in Christ's promises
         bring you peace.

> *You will keep in perfect peace*
> *him whose mind is steadfast,*
> *because he trusts in you.*
> ISAIAH 26:3

☐ 5 Comfort comes in knowing
          death is not the end.
     Those who die in Christ
          will live eternally.

> *Death has been swallowed up in victory.*
> *Thanks be to God! He gives us the*
> *victory through our Lord Jesus Christ.*
> 1 CORINTHIANS 15:54, 57

.... ℘ ....

☐ 6 May the memories of your loved one . . .
          of happy times,
          of joyful smiles,
          of hearty laughter,
          and caring words
     Help you through this sorrowful time.

> *Whatever is true, whatever is noble,*
> *whatever is right, whatever is pure,*
> *whatever is lovely, whatever is*
> *admirable—if anything is excellent or*
> *praiseworthy—think about such things.*
> PHILIPPIANS 4:8

As you grieve.
God has promised
  that comfort will come,
  that peace will be restored,
  that tears will eventually cease.

> *He will wipe every tear from their eyes. There will be no more death or mourning or crying or pain, for the old order of things has passed away.*
> Revelation 21:4

.... ✤ ....

Your loved one was a joy to know
  and a shining example
    of Christ's love.
My deepest sympathy
  for your great loss.

> *In my Father's house are many rooms; if it were not so, I would have told you. I am going there to prepare a place for you.*
> John 14:2

❑ 9   God's ways
        are sometimes mysterious.
    We do not understand
            this pain and loss,
        but we trust and have faith
            that God's way is perfect.
    With deepest sympathy.

> *In all things God works for the*
> *good of those who love him.*
> ROMANS 8:28

.... ✲ ....

❑ 10 Your pain and sorrow are shared
        by family and friends.
    May you find comfort
        in knowing so many care.
    My thoughts and prayers
        are with you.

> *Blessed are those who mourn,*
> *for they will be comforted.*
> MATTHEW 5:4

✺ SYMPATHY ✺
Record of Sentiments Sent

Note No.	Sent to:	Date

Sympathy—Loss of a Baby or Child

1. We do not know God's reasons, but our trust
   is in Him.
   With deepest sympathy on the loss of your baby.

> *Trust in the Lord with all your heart*
> *and lean not on your own understanding.*
> PROVERBS 3:5

2. We have no words to express how much we grieve
   for your sorrow.
   Our hearts are heavy and our thoughts are with you
   as you mourn the loss of your new baby.
   With deepest sympathy.

> *I wait for the Lord,*
> *my soul waits,*
> *And in his word*
> *I put my hope.*
> PSALM 130:5

We sorrow with you in the loss of this little life and
all the dreams left unfulfilled.
May it comfort you to know we care so much.

> *Because of the Lord's great love*
> *we are not consumed,*
> *for his compassions never fail.*
> *They are new every morning;*
> *great is your faithfulness.*
> LAMENTATIONS 3:22–23

.... ❧ ....

God has promised:
Tears and sorrow will end.
Comfort will come.
Peace will be restored.
And joy will be renewed.
With deepest sympathy on the loss of your child.

> *The Sovereign Lord will wipe*
> *away the tears from all faces.*
> ISAIAH 25:8

☐ 5   As you mourn for your baby.
         May God's love enfold you,
         May His peace surround you
Even as you face this most difficult time.

> *Come near to God and*
> *he will come near to you.*
> JAMES 4:8

··································· ·࿐· ···································

SYMPATHY—LOSS OF A BABY OR CHILD
Record of Sentiments Sent

Note No.	Sent to:	Date

Sympathy—Loss of a Spouse

❏ 1   God's ways are mysterious.
You may not understand this pain and loss,
You may question why your loved one is gone,
But I hope you find comfort in knowing God's way
   is perfect.
With sympathy on the loss of your husband [wife].

> *In all things God works for the*
> *good of those who love him.*
> ROMANS 8:28

.... ॐ ....

❏ 2   We sorrow with you in the death of your wife
   [husband].
Your pain and sorrow are shared by family and
   friends.
I hope you find comfort in knowing so many
   others care.

> *My comfort in my suffering is this:*
> *Your promise preserves my life.*
> PSALM 119:50

In your sorrow and loss, 3 ▢
 May God's presence bring you comfort
 and peace.

> *The Lord himself goes before you*
> *and will be with you; he will never*
> *leave you nor forsake you. Do not be*
> *afraid; do not be discouraged."*
> DEUTERONOMY 31:8

····························· ⁊ ·····························

You are in my thoughts and prayers as you grieve. 4 ▢
God bless you and keep you close in your time of
sadness and loss.

> *Be merciful to me, Lord, for I am faint;*
> *O Lord, heal me, for my bones are in agony.*
> *Turn, O Lord, and deliver me;*
> *save me because of your unfailing love.*
> PSALM 6:2,4

❑ 5   Faith is our comfort as we grieve.
       May your faith in Christ's promises bring you
           peace at this very sad time in your life.

*I have told you these things, so that
in me you may have peace.
In this world you will have trouble. But
take heart! I have overcome the world.*
JOHN 16:33

·· ⮥ ··

❑ 6   We mourn with you in the death of your wife
           [husband].
       She [he] was a joy to know and a shining example
           of Christ's love.
       We will miss her [him] too.
       In Christian sympathy and love.

*Let us then approach the throne of
grace with confidence, so that we
may receive mercy and find grace to
help us in our time of need.*
HEBREWS 4:16

ᔰ SYMPATHY—LOSS OF A SPOUSE ᔰ
Record of Sentiments Sent

Note No.	Sent to:	Date

Worth the Risk

❦

If we build more windows and fewer walls we will have more friends.

—Alan Loy McGinnis, *The Friendship Factor*

When we trust another person enough to tell her who we really are and how we really feel, we have shared our most precious possession. But for many of us, such openness seems like the ultimate risk. We feel vulnerable. What if we are taken lightly, belittled, betrayed, rudely corrected, abandoned, or rejected? Painful experiences flash their warning lights within us: *Danger! Do not enter!*

Such fears can give us a healthy sense of caution about indiscriminately stripping bare our soul to total strangers, or to people who have not shown themselves to be trustworthy. From such experiences we can learn the wisdom of a gradual process of discovery and disclosure.

But caution has gone beyond discretion when it keeps us closed off from others, living in fear of revealing who, what, and where we are. For not only is it healthy, right, and good to know and be known as we go through life, but there will inevitably come a time when we desperately need the ministry of someone who already understands and loves us.

One day I was sitting on the floor, working on a project with a friend. She seemed unusually quiet and withdrawn. Sensing trouble and not wanting my friend to suffer an internal explosion that could do serious damage when there would be no one around to administer first aid, I began to probe gently. At my subtle inquiries, she dodged and slid sideways, so I let it go and we continued our work.

During a break, I leaned against the wall, drew my legs to my chest, rested my chin on my knees, and began to share an area of need that could have made me vulnerable to her judgment. She listened with empathy, expressed her support, and finally said, "You shared that with me so that I'd be able to talk about what's wrong, didn't you?"

"Who, *me*?" I laughed, and then grew serious as her pain tumbled out in a heartrending torrent.

Later her world fell apart, and I will never forget what she said: "I'm so glad I shared with you before. I don't have to explain anything now. You already know. You see, I *couldn't* explain anything now. I'd have been *alone* in this. . . ."

Through openness, we had built a bridge of friendship that she could run across in a crisis—

run to understanding, comfort, caring, and help. An emergency is not a time to start a building project.

Keep on living an open, transparent life, because that is where the Spirit blooms and produces fruit in authentic relationships and demonstrates the kind of life God approves.

As we continue to share honestly with each other, we help one another grow to our full potential as Christians in unity with Christ our head. As each of us stays in union and harmony with Christ, we are energized and consequently give energy to others through Christ, enabling them in their growth and giving love to the family as a whole.

Discover new ways of expressing your new, unique personhood in Christ, ways which are in harmony with who you really are . . . This new behavior will demonstrate that you have a right relationship with yourself and with God and are becoming a whole person. Stop playing games, and be straight in your communication, because we are all dependent on each other. —Ephesians 5:8–10; 4:15–16, 24–25 (from *The Heart of Paul: A Relational Paraphrase of the New Testament* by Ben Campbell Johnson)

ॐ

SUSAN LENZKES
Crossing the Bridge Between You and Me

New Baby

□ 1 One small new life—
But oh, what surprises will unfold
   in the years to come!

> *Every good and perfect gift*
> *is from above.*
> JAMES 1:17

.... ⌇ ....

□ 2 Made in God's image
   Born in His love
A baby—God's wonder,
   His gift from above.

> *In the image of God*
> *has God made man.*
> GENESIS 9:6

Gazing into a newborn's eyes,
one sees the face of God.

3

> *The Lord bless you and keep you;*
> *The Lord make his face shine upon you*
> *and be gracious to you;*
> *The Lord turn his face toward you*
> *and give you peace.*
> NUMBERS 6:24–26

················· ❧ ·················

A new baby reminds us
of what wonderful gifts
God sends us.
Congratulations
on your new little one.

> *I praise you because*
> *I am fearfully and wonderfully made;*
> *your works are wonderful,*
> *I know that full well.*
> PSALM 139:14

☐ 5 Joy and happiness,
Laughter and fun
All await you as you enjoy watching you new baby
   thrive.
May God richly bless you and your new baby.

> *And whoever welcomes a little child like*
> *this in my name welcomes me.*
> MATTHEW 18:5

.... ☙ ....

☐ 6 What a wonderful gift God has given your family.
God bless you as you welcome this new baby to
   your home.
Congratulations on your new baby.

> *I prayed for this child, and the Lord has*
> *granted me what I asked of him.*
> 1 SAMUEL 1:27

Enjoy each moment and treasure each step of 7 ☐
watching your little one grow.
God's blessings on you and your new baby.

> *"Do you hear what these children*
> *are saying?" they asked him.*
> *"Yes," replied Jesus, "have you never read,*
> *" 'From the lips of children and infants*
> *you have ordained praise'?"*
> MATTHEW 21:16

.... ༉ ....

A baby is a gift that is full of surprises. 8 ☐
The yawns and giggles, the smiles that last,
Treasure each moment since they go by so fast.
Congratulations on your new baby.

> *Every good and perfect gift is*
> *from above, coming down from the*
> *Father of the heavenly lights.*
> JAMES 1:17

☐ 9 There is no gift so precious, there is no gift so
          sweet,
       As a bundle of a baby—two hands, bright eyes,
          small feet.
       Congratulations on your new bundle of joy.

> *The God who made the world and*
> *everything in it is the Lord of heaven*
> *and earth . . . he himself gives all men*
> *life and breath and everything else.*
> ACTS 17:24–25

✥ NEW BABY ✥
Record of Sentiments Sent

Note No.	Sent to:	Date

Adoption

◻ 1   Congratulations.
All God's children are His special little ones.
May God richly bless you and your new daughter
  [son] as you welcome her [him] into
  your arms, your home, your hearts.

> *I praise you because I am*
> *fearfully and wonderfully made;*
> *your works are wonderful,*
> *I know that full well.*
> PSALM 139:14

.... ॐ ....

◻ 2   "Jesus loves the little children, all the children of
  the world."
May you be an instrument of God's love and peace
  as you welcome His child into your home.

> *May the God of hope fill you with all*
> *joy and peace as you trust in him, so*
> *that you may overflow with hope by*
> *the power of the Holy Spirit.*
> ROMANS 15:13

I'm so glad God brought this special child into
   your life.
May you find that she [he] is the special gift God
   made all His children to be.

> *Every good and perfect gift is
> from above, coming down from the
> Father of the heavenly lights.*
> JAMES 1:17

.... ༄ ....

May God's love fill your lives as you open your
   hearts and your home to your adopted child.
God's blessings on your whole family.

> *The Lord bless you and keep you;
> the Lord make his face shine upon you
> and be gracious to you;
> the Lord turn his face toward you
> and give you peace.*
> NUMBERS 6:24–26

☐ 5 How wonderful that God has called you to adopt
a child.
May love, tenderness, and caring unite you as a
family.

> *For it is God who works in you to will and*
> *to act according to his good purpose.*
> PHILIPPIANS 2:13

.... ✺ ....

☐ 6 I'm so proud that you are a family who has chosen
to welcome a child into your home.
May God richly bless your lives as you love and
nurture your little one.

> *You will eat the fruit of your labor;*
> *blessings and prosperity will be yours.*
> PSALM 128:2

God calls us to do great things for Him.
Being asked to love a child from a different home
    and culture is one of His best assignments.
May you be blessed through this experience of
    adopting a little one into your family.

> *And whatever you do, whether in*
> *word or deed, do it all in the name*
> *of the Lord Jesus, giving thanks to*
> *God the Father through him.*
> COLOSSIANS 3:17

✌ ADOPTION ✌
Record of Sentiments Sent

Note No.	Sent to:	Date

Dedication

As your baby is dedicated, may you realize that   1
    God holds your little one close in His arms.
He will protect and provide for her [him] wherever
    she [he] goes.

> *"For I know the plans I have for you,"*
> *declares the LORD, "plans to prosper you and*
> *not to harm you, plans to give you hope and a*
> *future. Then you will call upon me and come*
> *and pray to me and I will listen to you."*
> JEREMIAH 29:11–12

God's blessings surround you,   2
His peace enfold you,
and His love go with your little one, on this day of
    dedication and for all the years to come.

> *Know that the LORD is God.*
> *It is he who made us, and we are his,*
> *we are his people, the sheep of his pasture.*
> PSALM 100:3

3 On this day that you dedicate your little one to God,
May you feel God's tenderness
and embrace His loving promise
that He will be with your child wherever he [she]
goes.

> *Jesus said, "Let the little children*
> *come to me, and do not hinder*
> *them, for the kingdom of heaven*
> *belongs to such as these."*
> MATTHEW 19:14

.... ૐ ....

4 May God shower you and your little one with His
blessings and surround you with His love on this
special day of dedication and in all the
years ahead.

> *How great is the love the Father has*
> *lavished on us, that we should be called*
> *children of God! And that is what we are!*
> 1 JOHN 3:1

A Prayer for Your Baby's Dedication:
Today, we dedicate this little one to you, O Lord.
Guide him [her] in the way he [she] should go.
Protect his [her] path and preserve his [her]
    every move.
Strengthen and encourage him [her] as he [she]
    discovers and uses the gifts you have given
        him [her].
Provide for his [her] every need and fill him [her]
    with your peace.

> *"Because he loves me," says the* LORD, *"I*
> *will rescue him; I will protect him, for*
> *he acknowledges my name."*
>
> PSALM 91:14

❧ DEDICATION ❧
Record of Sentiments Sent

Note No.	Sent to:	Date

Wedding

In your new life together,
    may your sorrows be few
    and your joys be as abundant
    as the sands of the seashore.

1 ☐

> *Satisfy us in the morning with*
> *your unfailing love,*
> *that we may sing for joy*
> *and be glad all our days.*
> PSALM 90:14

· 〜 ·

Your marriage—
    two lives
    united in Christ
    and surrounded by God's love.

2 ☐

> *The Lord bless you and keep you;*
> *The Lord make his face shine upon you*
> *and be gracious to you;*
> *The Lord turn his face toward you and*
> *give you peace.*
> NUMBERS 6:24–26

☐ 3   May the hopes and dreams
        you hold in your hearts today
        be fulfilled in
            your lifetime together.

> *Commit to the Lord whatever you do,*
> *and your plans will succeed.*
> PROVERBS 16:3

.... ⌒ ....

☐ 4   May God's love surround you,
        His peace enfold you,
        His faithfulness guard you
            throughout your life together.

> *Live a life of love,*
> *just as Christ loved us.*
> EPHESIANS 5:2

May your love deepen
  through the years
And your joys multiply
  in your life together.

> *[Love] always protects, always trusts,*
> *always hopes, always perseveres.*
> *Love never fails.*
> 1 CORINTHIANS 13:7–8

.... ♪ ....

⟆ WEDDING ⟆
Record of Sentiments Sent

Note No.	Sent to:	Date

Anniversary

A marriage with God at its center   1 ☐
   will last a lifetime.
Congratulations on your
   exemplary life together.

> *For this God is our God*
> *for ever and ever;*
> *he will be our guide*
> *even to the end.*
> PSALM 48:14

.... ☙ ....

Happy Anniversary.   2 ☐
   It's a day to remember
      the love you've shared
And to rejoice in the joy
   you've known throughout the years!
Congratulations!

> *Now these three remain:*
> *faith, hope and love.*
> *But the greatest of these is love.*
> 1 CORINTHIANS 13:13

☐ 3　Though the memories and
　　　photos of your wedding day
　　　may fade with time,
　　Your love for one another
　　　continues to shine brightly
　　　with each new day.
　　Congratulations on
　　　your wedding anniversary.

[Love] always protects,
always trusts, always hopes,
always perseveres.
1 CORINTHIANS 13:7

·································· ✌ ··································

☐ 4　Today is the day to celebrate
　　　the love you share as a couple
　　And the joy your life together
　　　has brought to so many others.
　　Happy Anniversary!

Live a life of love,
just as Christ loved us.
EPHESIANS 5:2

Your anniversary is the perfect day
    to celebrate your life of love.
Congratulations!

He who pursues righteousness and love
finds life, prosperity
and honor.

PROVERBS 21:21

················· ɔ ·················

✌ ANNIVERSARY ✌
Record of Sentiments Sent

Note No.	Sent to:	Date

Addresses and Special Dates

NAME: _____

ADDRESS: _____

ANNIVERSARY _____ BIRTHDAY: _____

ADDITIONAL INFORMATION: _____

_____

_____

NAME: _____

ADDRESS: _____

ANNIVERSARY _____ BIRTHDAY: _____

ADDITIONAL INFORMATION: _____

_____

_____

NAME: _____

ADDRESS: _____

ANNIVERSARY _____ BIRTHDAY: _____

ADDITIONAL INFORMATION: _____

_____

_____

NAME: _____

ADDRESS: _____

ANNIVERSARY _____ BIRTHDAY: _____

ADDITIONAL INFORMATION: _____

_____

_____

NAME: _____

ADDRESS: _____

ANNIVERSARY _____ BIRTHDAY: _____

ADDITIONAL INFORMATION: _____

_____

_____

NAME: _____

ADDRESS: _____

ANNIVERSARY _____ BIRTHDAY: _____

ADDITIONAL INFORMATION: _____

_____

_____

NAME: _____

ADDRESS: _____

ANNIVERSARY _____ BIRTHDAY: _____

ADDITIONAL INFORMATION: _____

_____

_____

NAME: _____

ADDRESS: _____

ANNIVERSARY _____ BIRTHDAY: _____

ADDITIONAL INFORMATION: _____

_____

_____

NAME: _____

ADDRESS: _____

ANNIVERSARY _____ BIRTHDAY: _____

ADDITIONAL INFORMATION: _____

_____

_____

NAME: _____

ADDRESS: _____

ANNIVERSARY _____ BIRTHDAY: _____

ADDITIONAL INFORMATION: _____

_____

_____

NAME: _____

ADDRESS: _____

ANNIVERSARY _____ BIRTHDAY: _____

ADDITIONAL INFORMATION: _____

_____

_____

NAME: _____

ADDRESS: _____

ANNIVERSARY _____ BIRTHDAY: _____

ADDITIONAL INFORMATION: _____

_____

_____

NAME: _____

ADDRESS: _____

ANNIVERSARY _____ BIRTHDAY: _____

ADDITIONAL INFORMATION: _____

_____

_____

NAME: _____

ADDRESS: _____

ANNIVERSARY _____ BIRTHDAY: _____

ADDITIONAL INFORMATION: _____

_____

_____

NAME: _____

ADDRESS: _____

ANNIVERSARY _____ BIRTHDAY: _____

ADDITIONAL INFORMATION: _____

_____

_____

NAME: _____

ADDRESS: _____

ANNIVERSARY _____ BIRTHDAY: _____

ADDITIONAL INFORMATION: _____

_____

_____

NAME: _____

ADDRESS: _____

ANNIVERSARY _____ BIRTHDAY: _____

ADDITIONAL INFORMATION: _____

_____

_____

NAME: _____

ADDRESS: _____

ANNIVERSARY _____ BIRTHDAY: _____

ADDITIONAL INFORMATION: _____

_____

_____

NAME: _____

ADDRESS: _____

ANNIVERSARY _____ BIRTHDAY: _____

ADDITIONAL INFORMATION: _____

_____

_____

NAME: _____

ADDRESS: _____

ANNIVERSARY _____ BIRTHDAY: _____

ADDITIONAL INFORMATION: _____

_____

_____

NAME: _____

ADDRESS: _____

ANNIVERSARY _____ BIRTHDAY: _____

ADDITIONAL INFORMATION: _____

_____

_____

NAME: _____

ADDRESS: _____

ANNIVERSARY _____ BIRTHDAY: _____

ADDITIONAL INFORMATION: _____

_____

_____

NAME: _____

ADDRESS: _____

ANNIVERSARY _____ BIRTHDAY: _____

ADDITIONAL INFORMATION: _____

_____

_____

NAME: _____

ADDRESS: _____

ANNIVERSARY _____ BIRTHDAY: _____

ADDITIONAL INFORMATION: _____

_____

_____

NAME: _____

ADDRESS: _____

ANNIVERSARY _____ BIRTHDAY: _____

ADDITIONAL INFORMATION: _____

_____

_____

NAME: _____

ADDRESS: _____

ANNIVERSARY _____ BIRTHDAY: _____

ADDITIONAL INFORMATION: _____

_____

_____

NAME: _____

ADDRESS: _____

ANNIVERSARY _____ BIRTHDAY: _____

ADDITIONAL INFORMATION: _____

_____

_____

NAME: _____

ADDRESS: _____

ANNIVERSARY _____ BIRTHDAY: _____

ADDITIONAL INFORMATION: _____

_____

_____

NAME: _____

ADDRESS: _____

ANNIVERSARY _____ BIRTHDAY: _____

ADDITIONAL INFORMATION: _____

_____

_____

NAME: _____

ADDRESS: _____

ANNIVERSARY _____ BIRTHDAY: _____

ADDITIONAL INFORMATION: _____

_____

_____

NAME: _____

ADDRESS: _____

ANNIVERSARY _____ BIRTHDAY: _____

ADDITIONAL INFORMATION: _____

_____

_____

NAME: _____

ADDRESS: _____

ANNIVERSARY _____ BIRTHDAY: _____

ADDITIONAL INFORMATION: _____

_____

_____

NAME: _____

ADDRESS: _____

ANNIVERSARY _____ BIRTHDAY: _____

ADDITIONAL INFORMATION: _____

_____

_____

NAME: _____

ADDRESS: _____

ANNIVERSARY _____ BIRTHDAY: _____

ADDITIONAL INFORMATION: _____

_____

_____

NAME: _____

ADDRESS: _____

ANNIVERSARY _____ BIRTHDAY: _____

ADDITIONAL INFORMATION: _____

_____

_____

NAME: _____

ADDRESS: _____

ANNIVERSARY _____ BIRTHDAY: _____

ADDITIONAL INFORMATION: _____

_____

_____

NAME: _____

ADDRESS: _____

ANNIVERSARY _____ BIRTHDAY: _____

ADDITIONAL INFORMATION: _____

_____

_____

NAME: _____

ADDRESS: _____

ANNIVERSARY _____ BIRTHDAY: _____

ADDITIONAL INFORMATION: _____

_____

_____

NAME: _____

ADDRESS: _____

ANNIVERSARY _____ BIRTHDAY: _____

ADDITIONAL INFORMATION: _____

_____

_____

NAME: _____

ADDRESS: _____

ANNIVERSARY _____ BIRTHDAY: _____

ADDITIONAL INFORMATION: _____

_____

_____

NAME: _____

ADDRESS: _____

ANNIVERSARY _____ BIRTHDAY: _____

ADDITIONAL INFORMATION: _____

_____

_____

NAME: _____

ADDRESS: _____

ANNIVERSARY _____ BIRTHDAY: _____

ADDITIONAL INFORMATION: _____

_____

_____

NAME: _____

ADDRESS: _____

ANNIVERSARY _____ BIRTHDAY: _____

ADDITIONAL INFORMATION: _____

_____

_____

NAME: _____

ADDRESS: _____

ANNIVERSARY _____ BIRTHDAY: _____

ADDITIONAL INFORMATION: _____

_____

_____

NAME: _____

ADDRESS: _____

ANNIVERSARY _____ BIRTHDAY: _____

ADDITIONAL INFORMATION: _____

_____

_____

NAME: _____

ADDRESS: _____

ANNIVERSARY _____ BIRTHDAY: _____

ADDITIONAL INFORMATION: _____

_____

_____

NAME: _____

ADDRESS: _____

ANNIVERSARY _____ BIRTHDAY: _____

ADDITIONAL INFORMATION: _____

_____

_____

NAME: _____

ADDRESS: _____

ANNIVERSARY _____ BIRTHDAY: _____

ADDITIONAL INFORMATION: _____

_____

_____

NAME: _____

ADDRESS: _____

ANNIVERSARY _____ BIRTHDAY: _____

ADDITIONAL INFORMATION: _____

_____

_____

NAME: _____

ADDRESS: _____

ANNIVERSARY _____ BIRTHDAY: _____

ADDITIONAL INFORMATION: _____

_____

_____

NAME: _____

ADDRESS: _____

ANNIVERSARY _____ BIRTHDAY: _____

ADDITIONAL INFORMATION: _____

_____

_____

NAME: _____

ADDRESS: _____

ANNIVERSARY _____ BIRTHDAY: _____

ADDITIONAL INFORMATION: _____

_____

_____

NAME: _____

ADDRESS: _____

ANNIVERSARY _____ BIRTHDAY: _____

ADDITIONAL INFORMATION: _____

_____

_____

NAME: _____

ADDRESS: _____

ANNIVERSARY _____ BIRTHDAY: _____

ADDITIONAL INFORMATION: _____

_____

_____

NAME: _____

ADDRESS: _____

ANNIVERSARY _____ BIRTHDAY: _____

ADDITIONAL INFORMATION: _____

_____

_____

NAME: _____

ADDRESS: _____

ANNIVERSARY _____ BIRTHDAY: _____

ADDITIONAL INFORMATION: _____

_____

_____

NAME: _____

ADDRESS: _____

ANNIVERSARY _____ BIRTHDAY: _____

ADDITIONAL INFORMATION: _____

_____

_____

— Note to the Reader —

The publisher invites you to share your response to the message of this book by writing Discovery House Publishers, P.O. Box 3566, Grand Rapids, MI 49501, U.S.A. For information about other Discovery House books, music, videos, or DVDs, contact us at the same address or call 1-800-653-8333. Find us on the Internet at http://www.dhp.org/ or send an e-mail to books@dhp.org.